JOHN LESLEY

THE WORLD'S GREATEST CITIES

SYDNEY

AUSTRALIA

REDBACK publishing

First Published 2024 by
Redback Publishing
Suite 6, 13a Narabang Way,
Belrose NSW 2085
Australia

www.redbackpublishing.com
info@redbackpublishing.com

ISBN 978-1-761400-77-3

Author: John Lesley
Editing: Caroline Thomas
Design: Redback Publishing

NATIONAL LIBRARY OF AUSTRALIA
A catalogue record for this book is available from the National Library of Australia

Originated by Redback Publishing

Acknowledgements
Abbreviations: l—left, r—right, b—bottom, t—top, c—centre, m—middle. We would like to thank the following for permission to reproduce photographs: Images © shutterstock;
Pg4t Natsicha Wetchasart / Shutterstock.com, pg6r SAKARET / Shutterstock.com, pg7tr cornfield / Shutterstock.com, pg9ml Kirsty Hulme Shutterstock.com, pg9tr National Library of Australia, pg10b arawut Konganantdech / Shutterstock-com, pg11br Umer Arif / Shutterstock.com, pg12 superjoseph / shutterstock.com, pg13b ArliftAtoz2205 / Shutterstock.com, pg14tl Regien Paassen / Shutterstock.com, pg14br singh_lens / Shutterstock.com, pg15tl HDC Creative / Shutterstock.com, pg16t aiyoshi597 / Shutterstock.com, pg18t Dixson Galleries, State Library of New South Wales, pg18b Mitchell Library, State Library of New South Wales, pg19t Mitchell Library, State Library of New South Wales, pg19b
Mitchell Library, State Library of New South Wales, pg20tl Petar B photography / Shutterstock.com, pg22bl ChameleonsEye / Shutterstock.com, pg23tr faithie / Shutterstock.com, pg25br Keitma / Shutterstock.com, pg26br Anton Ukolov / Shutterstock.com, pg27br Rose Marinelli / Shutterstock.com, pg28bl Fimina Anna / Shutterstock.com, pg29 br Olga Kashubin / Shutterstock.com, pg32ml Paulharding00 / Shutterstock.com, pg32tr girlwander1982 / Shutterstock.com,

CONTENTS

SYDNEY QUICK FACTS

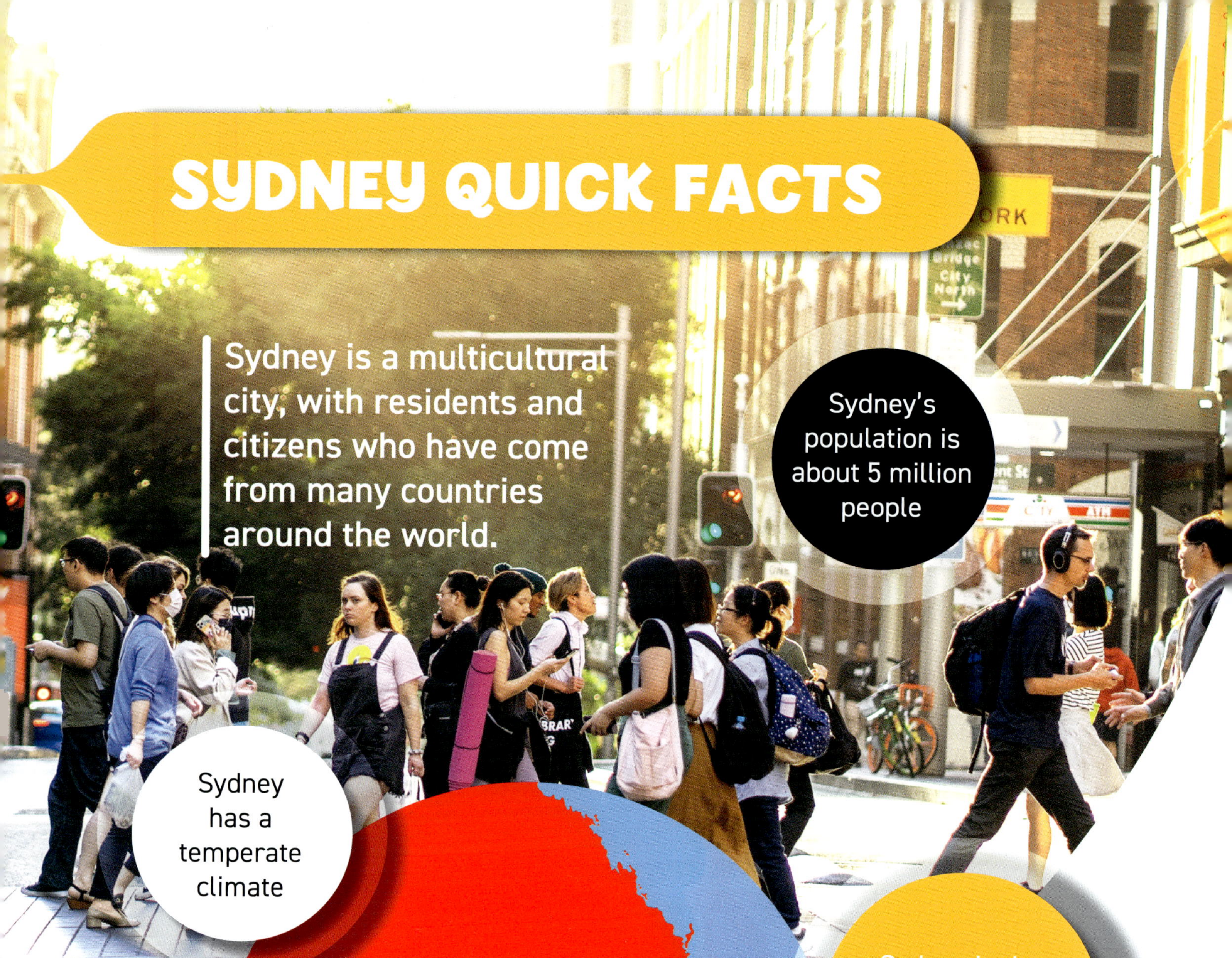

Sydney is a multicultural city, with residents and citizens who have come from many countries around the world.

Sydney's population is about 5 million people

Sydney has a temperate climate

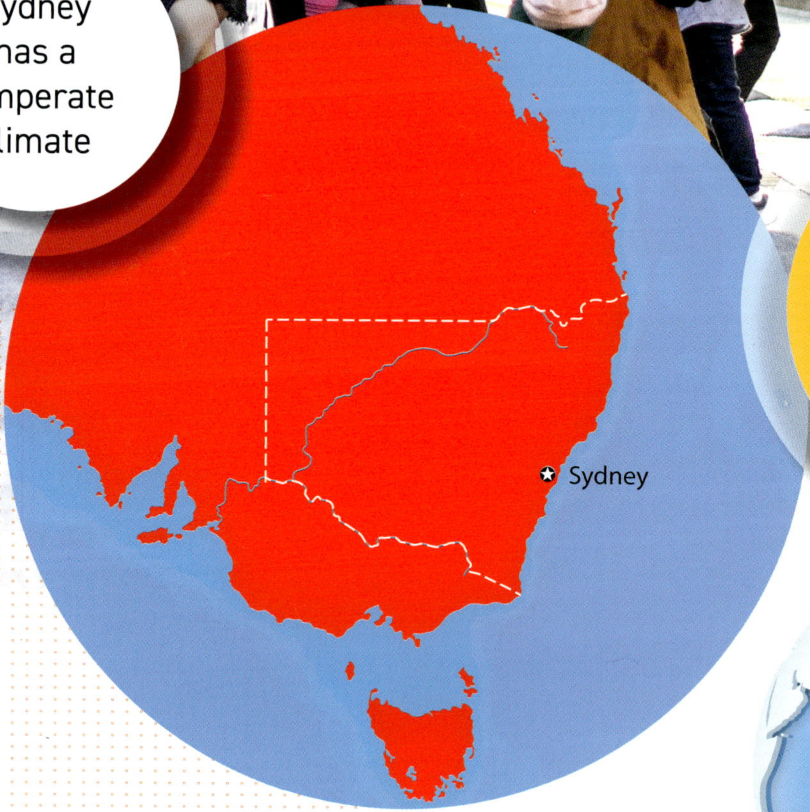

Sydney is the capital city of the Australian state of New South Wales

SYDNEY'S GEOGRAPHY

Sydney is located on the southeast coast of Australia. Although the main business centre of Sydney sits on the shores of a beautiful harbour, Sydney's sprawling suburbs extend across a large, flat basin.

The Blue Mountains, which are part of the Great Dividing Range, mark the western boundary of Sydney.

Large expanses of sandstone form the base on which the city of Sydney is built. This sandstone was quarried and used by the early colonists to construct many buildings which are still standing throughout Sydney and its suburbs.

SYDNEY HARBOUR

The blue waters of Sydney's large harbour are shared by seagoing ships, recreational boaters and swimmers. Surrounding the harbour are many beaches, some of them crowded and others only visited by the few locals who know where they are.

SYDNEY HARBOUR 10,000 YEARS AGO

The harbour was formed thousands of years ago at the end of the last Ice Age. The Parramatta River once ran through a deep valley towards the Pacific Ocean. When sea levels rose due to melting ice, the river was flooded, creating a harbour with many bays and inlets.

INDIGENOUS PEOPLE OF SYDNEY

Australian Aboriginal people have lived on the Australian continent for at least 65,000 years. The Sydney area was home to many Aboriginal people when the British first arrived in 1788.

- Image from the Bicentennial $10 note

BENNELONG

Sydney Opera House stands on Bennelong Point, which was named after Bennelong, a local Wangal man. A friendship developed between Governor Phillip and Bennelong, who became a cultural ambassador for the local Aboriginal people. Bennelong lived on Bennelong Point for a while in a brick hut that the Governor had built for him in 1791.

EORA - The City of Sydney area
DHARUG - From the harbour to western Sydney
DHARAWAL - Southern Sydney
GURINGAI - Northern Sydney

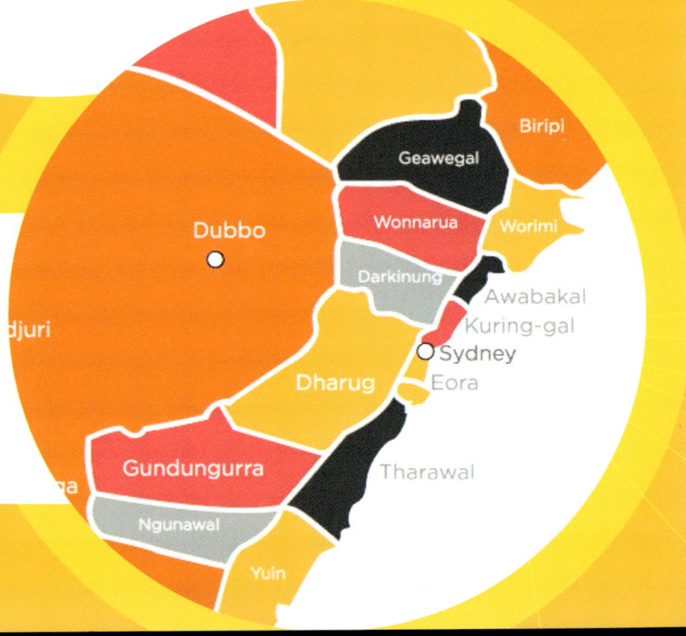

SYDNEY'S HISTORY

Sydney was founded by the British on 26 January, 1788. The First Fleet of eleven ships brought about 1,500 convicts and their guards to create a new town as a prison colony.

After years of struggling to feed themselves, despite the wealth of food sources all around them, the new arrivals eventually began to farm the land. As they extended their claim on the forests, cutting them down to create fields, the Aboriginal people lost more and more of their territory.

UNESCO WORLD HERITAGE SITES IN SYDNEY

COCKATOO ISLAND IN SYDNEY HARBOUR

Cockatoo Island is the largest island in Sydney Harbour. The underground, stone bins that convicts built on Cockatoo Island were used to store grain. The bins kept out vermin and also protected the stores from theft. From 1857 to 1992, Cockatoo Island was the site of a shipbuilding and repair industry.

OLD GOVERNMENT HOUSE AT PARRAMATTA

Government House at Parramatta was built as a country residence where the Governors went to escape the poor water supply and lack of proper sanitation in Sydney. Government House dates from 1790, although another building was on the same site even before this date.

HYDE PARK BARRACKS IN SYDNEY

Now a museum, these barracks once housed convicts. The building was designed by convict architect Francis Greenway in 1819.

Begun in 1956 and opened in 1973, the Sydney Opera House has become an iconic symbol of Australia. The Danish architect, Jørn Utzon, won an international competition for the design of the new opera house. Most of the funding for construction came from public lotteries.

SYDNEY OPERA HOUSE ON BENNELONG POINT IN SYDNEY

GOING TO SCHOOL IN SYDNEY

• Sydney University

Going to school is compulsory for children in Sydney from the ages of six to seventeen. There is a wide range of school types, including public and private, as well as religion-based schools.

HOLIDAYS

Sydney's schools have four terms per year, with the longest holidays being over the Christmas period.

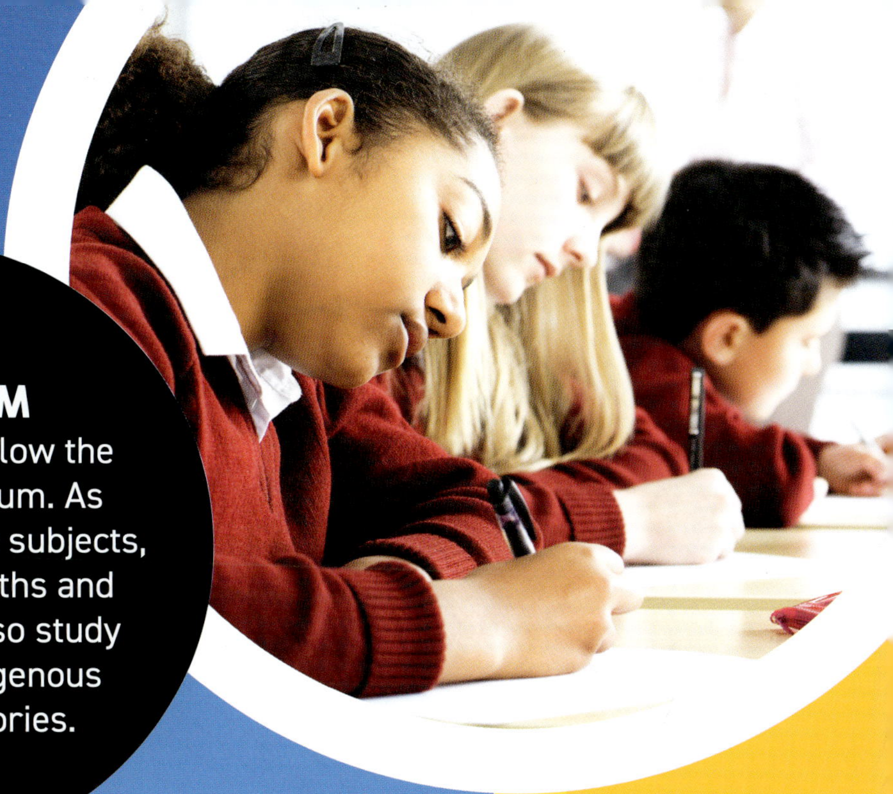

CURRICULUM

All schools must follow the Australian Curriculum. As well as learning basic subjects, such as English, maths and science, students also study the Australian Indigenous cultures and histories.

UNIVERSITIES

Sydney's Universities are amongst the best in the world and attract many international students. The fees paid by these students are an important source of government revenue.

SPORT IN SYDNEY

Olympic stadium Sydney

SYDNEY OLYMPIC GAMES

Australia prides itself on being a sporting nation. When the Sydney Olympics were held in 2000, sports facilities throughout Sydney were greatly enhanced. Juan Antonio Samaranch, President of the International Olympic Committee, proclaimed the Sydney event *"the best Olympic Games ever"*.

Sydney Cricket Ground

THE SYDNEY CRICKET GROUND

The history of the SCG goes back to the mid-1800s, when soldiers from the nearby Victoria Barracks played cricket on a pitch that they cleared themselves.

Since then, the SCG has become a revered ground where fans can see their favourite sporting stars in action.

Dragon boat racing

WATER SPORTS

Being a harbour city allows Sydneysiders to spend time enjoying water sports. The numerous beaches provide opportunities for surfing and swimming, and the harbour and rivers are magnets for people who love to sail or use powered vessels.

Royal National Park

BUSHWALKING

Even though there are millions of people living across Sydney, there are still many places where bushwalkers can enjoy the tranquility of eucalypt forests and the views that only a bushwalker can discover.

SYDNEY'S POPULATION

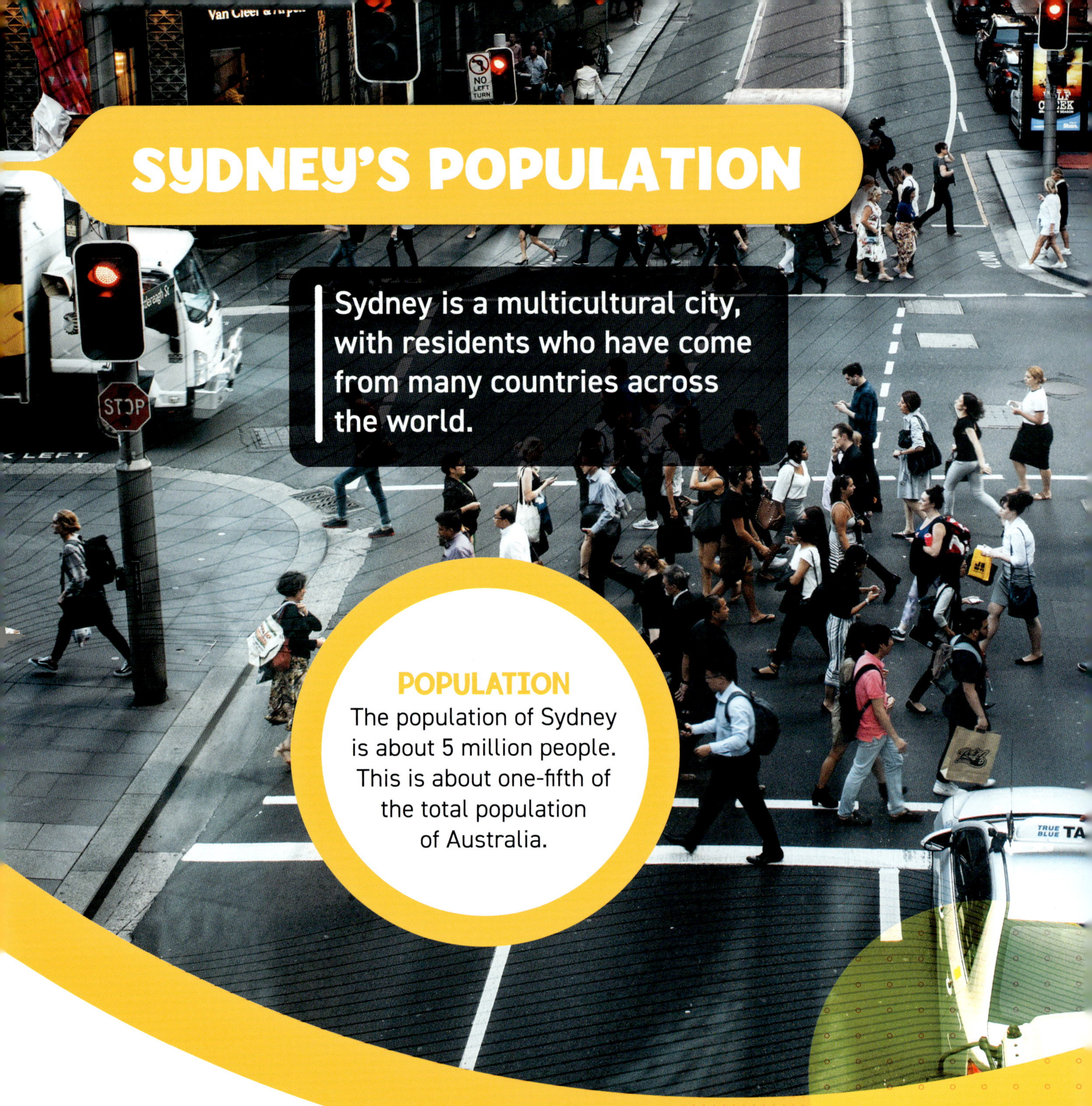

Sydney is a multicultural city, with residents who have come from many countries across the world.

POPULATION

The population of Sydney is about 5 million people. This is about one-fifth of the total population of Australia.

IMMIGRATION

Ever since it was founded in 1788, Sydney has depended on immigration for its development and growth. Most of the early settlers were British, but there were also settlers from other European and Middle Eastern countries, and from Asia.

SUBURBS

The majority of Sydneysiders live in the suburbs that extend for kilometres from the city centre.

CULTURES

Chinese immigrants developed their own Chinatown in the heart of Sydney.

Greek immigrants ran restaurants, milk-bars and factories throughout Sydney.

Italian immigrants settled around Leichhardt, not far from the centre of Sydney.

TRANSPORT IN SYDNEY

EARLY ROADS

The British settlers began clearing tracks and building roads almost as soon as they arrived in 1788. The major roads were laid out in a standard north-south and east-west pattern, and named after important people both in Britain and in the colony.

• Corner of George and Hunter Streets, ca. 1849

WATERWAYS

Clearing the bush to make way for roads was hard work and needed a lot of labourers. For a long time, the settlers and colonists used boats to travel from one place to another around Sydney. This form of travel was faster and safer than trying to make their way through thick bushland.

INDIGENOUS PEOPLE

The Indigenous people of Sydney had paths and tracks throughout the area. They also used canoes to travel to islands in the harbour and along rivers.

First Government House, Sydney 1807

Wollongong 1800s

HORSES AND OXEN

Before there were any cars or trucks, horses and oxen were the only sources of power that could be used to move heavy freight around Sydney. Convicts pulled carts full of stone and wood, but they were not as strong as animals, and they were also on the verge of starvation during the early years of settlement.

THE AGE OF STEAM

The invention of the steam engine was an innovation as important as electric vehicles and maglev trains are today. The first steam trains ran in Sydney in the mid-1800s, and steam-powered ferries made travel around Sydney harbour much faster.

Steam locomotive, Thirlmere

MODERN TRANSPORT

Any large city needs a varied and reliable transport system. Sydneysiders use cars, buses, trains, trams, light rail, ferries and other types of boats to travel around their city. Bicycle paths are a feature that many local government councils provide for both recreation and commuting.

Tram in Sydney CBD

SYDNEY AT WORK

Sydney's suburbs were once full of manufacturing industries and factories of all types. In recent years, the level of manufacturing has decreased. The leading industries in Sydney are now involved in finance, tourism, education and professional or social services.

Old industrial building

Some people commute to and from the Central Business District, or CBD, in the city each day for work, but many people work in suburban centres all across Greater Sydney.

FOOD AND FARMS

FARMS

Even though Sydney is a large, global city, it still has some outlying areas devoted to food production and farming. A large proportion of Sydney's eggs, poultry and vegetables comes from local farms.

FISHING

People engaged in the fishing industry use berths all around Sydney Harbour. The biggest fish market in the southern hemisphere is located in Blackwattle Bay, in Pyrmont, Sydney. Recreational fishing is a popular activity along the coast and in rivers around Sydney.

Sydney Fish Market

SYDNEY HARBOUR BRIDGE

Known locally as the coat hanger, Sydney Harbour Bridge connects the southern and northern shores of the city. Before it was opened in 1932, a ferry carried passengers from one side of the harbour to the other. A tunnel under the harbour was opened in 1992 to carry the increasing amount of road traffic.

• Sydney Harbour Bridge

THE ROCKS

Cadmans Cottage, one of the oldest buildings in Sydney

The Rocks is an historic precinct near the harbour in Sydney. Buildings in The Rocks are amongst the oldest in Sydney, and they form an area of colonial style buildings that is unique in the city.

CHINATOWN

Chinese migrants have been coming to Sydney to work since the earliest days of the colony. They tended to congregate in one part of the city, near the docks and waterfront. This area is now a thriving Chinatown.

CIRCULAR QUAY

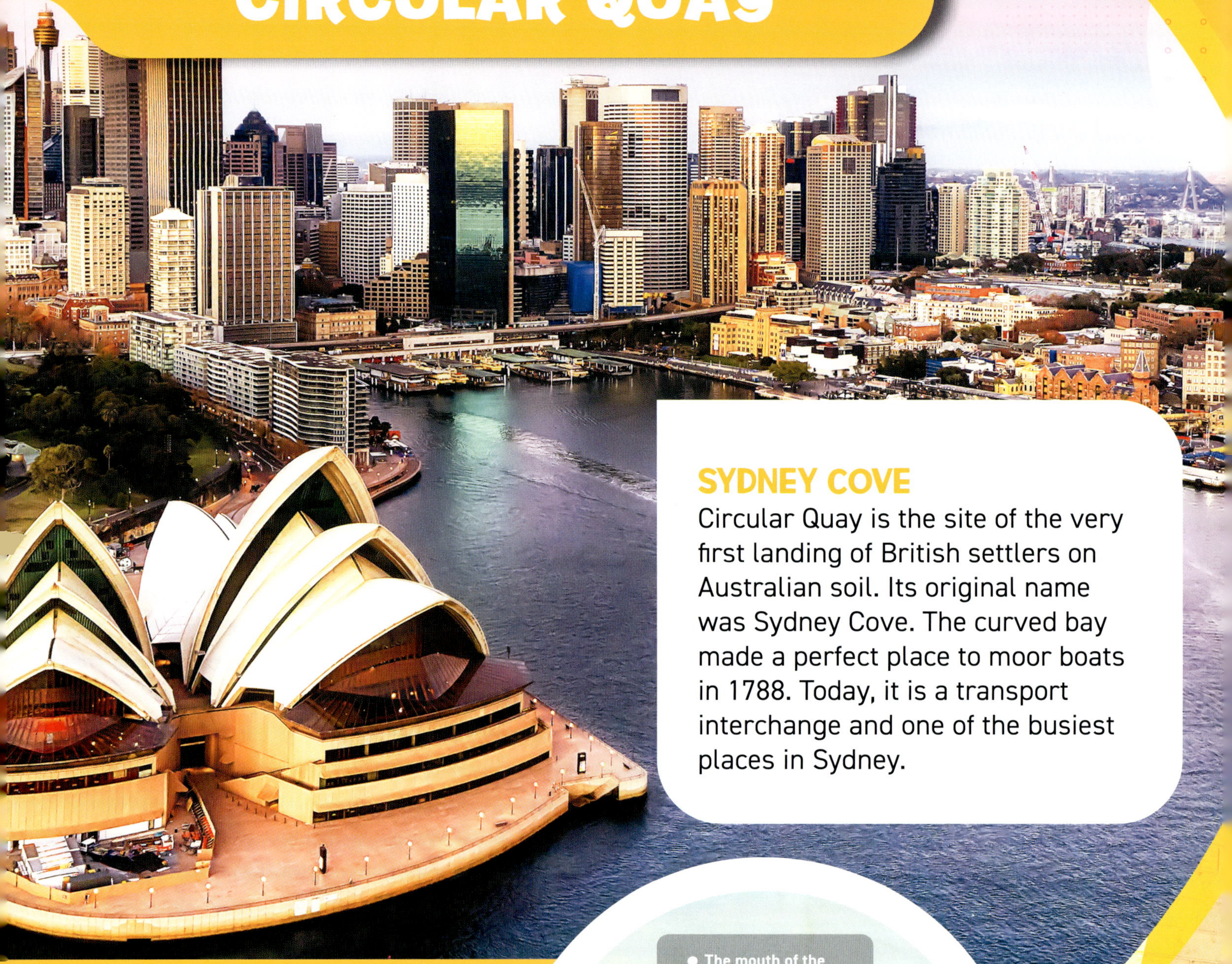

SYDNEY COVE

Circular Quay is the site of the very first landing of British settlers on Australian soil. Its original name was Sydney Cove. The curved bay made a perfect place to moor boats in 1788. Today, it is a transport interchange and one of the busiest places in Sydney.

The mouth of the Tank Stream in Sydney Cove, 1803

TANK STREAM

The settlers' fresh water originally came from a small stream that flowed into Sydney Cove. They called it the Tank Stream. It still exists, but is now hidden in pipes under the ground.

PARLIAMENT HOUSE

Macquarie Street in Sydney is the location of Parliament House. The historic building began its life as the Rum Hospital, so named because the workers who built it were paid in rum rather than with money.

Sydney early 1800s

SYDNEY'S BEACHES

There are over 100 beaches in Sydney, including two of Australia's most famous beaches: Manly Beach and Bondi Beach.

Manly Beach

MANLY BEACH

Named by Governor Phillip in 1788 because of the confidence of the Indigenous men he saw there, Manly Beach is now a tourist hot-spot. Manly allows access to a surf beach on one side and a harbour beach on the other, both connected by a pedestrian mall. Manly has been a popular place to visit since the 1850s.

• Bondi Beach

BONDI BEACH

The world's first surf lifesaving club opened at Bondi Beach in the early 1900s. Up until the late 1800s, Bondi Beach was private land.

OTHER BEACHES

Beaches all around the harbour and along the Pacific Ocean coastline give Sydneysiders many places to choose from when they want a day at the beach.

ROYAL BOTANIC GARDEN

This botanical garden is right in the heart of Sydney. Its magnificent location on the shores of the harbour makes it a perfect place to escape from the city, which is just a short stroll away.

In 1788, the area was the site of the first farm where the settlers attempted to grow their own food.

GLOSSARY

ambassador person who represents their people to others

berth where a boat or ship is moored

curriculum subjects studied for a course

facility place and equipment provided for special uses

lottery game of chance based on winning something

mall place where people can walk and shop

multicultural having features from many different cultures

pedestrian referring to people who are walking

proclaim declare to the public

quarry to take stone or other substances from the ground

revered admired and respected

sanitation provision of clean water and sewerage

sprawling spreading out in many directions

temperate climate mild climate

tranquillity peacefulness

vermin creatures that are destructive and cause disease

INDEX

Hyde Park Barracks